MARGARET OF ATHENS

A One Only Collection

Art And Jewelry

Book Two

SOLD

9

Model is Mom! Willie Mae Simmons

Howdy Hat Band

A collective

Another Collection

Sandstone And Faux Pearls

Portrait of Bill Simmons
Painted 1985

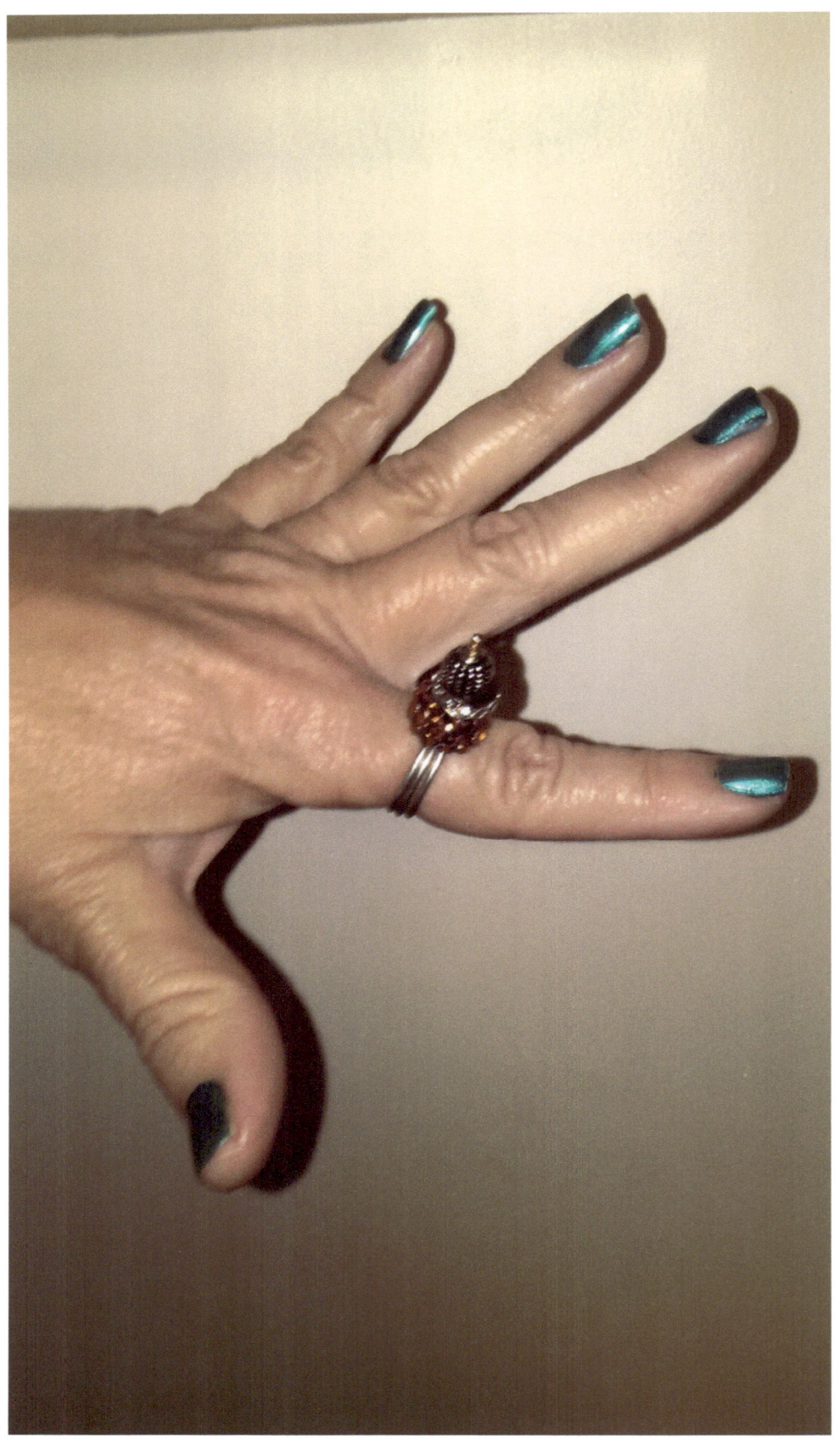

Wall Mural

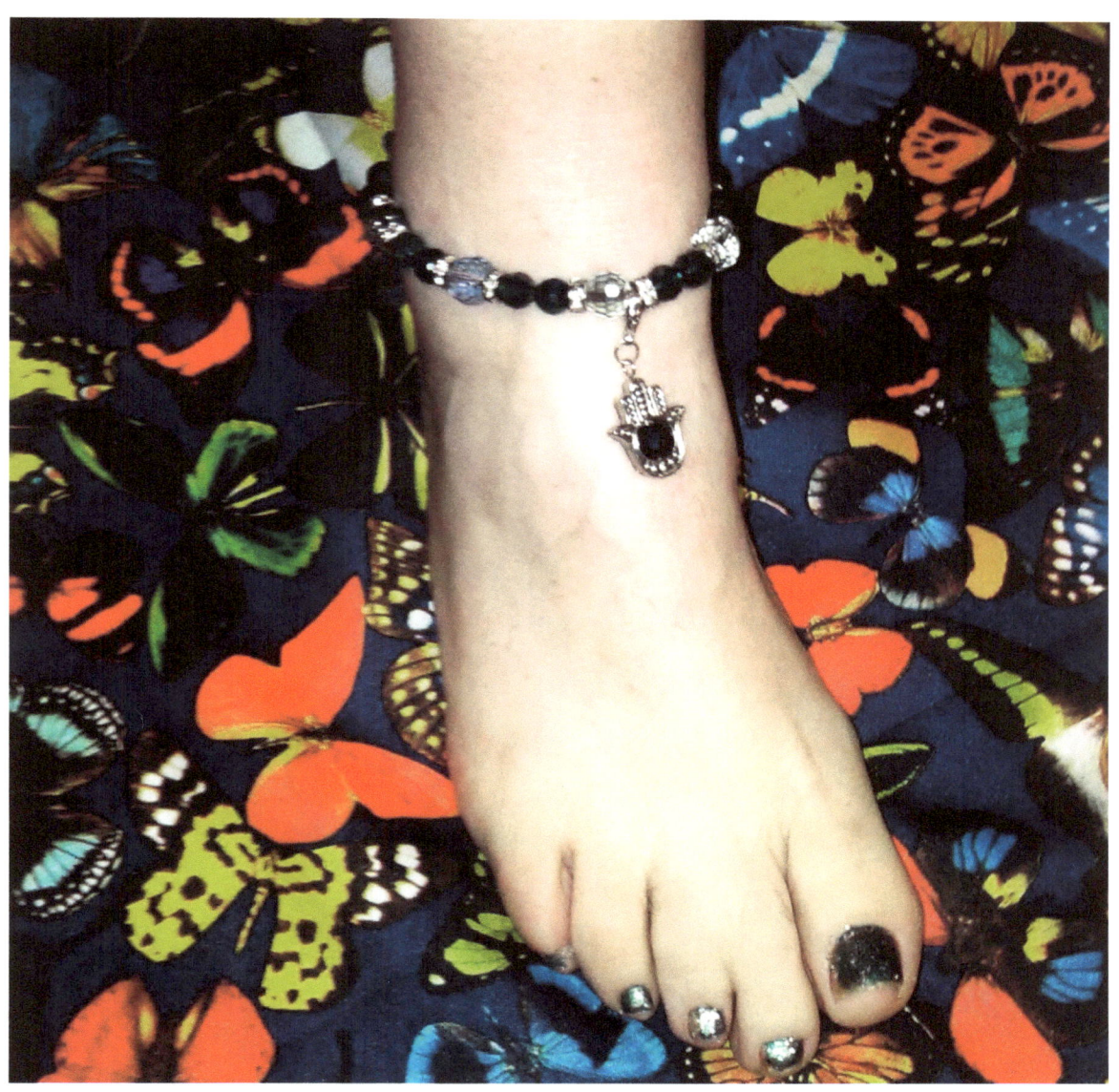

Anklet

Cherry Bracelet

My supporting staff!